MEDITATIONS
— ON —
# SILENCE

SISTER
WENDY BECKETT

DORLING KINDERSLEY
LONDON • NEW YORK • STUTTGART

A DORLING KINDERSLEY BOOK

*For Sister Ann Marie, O.CARM,
who looks after me with such charity.*

Editor *Patricia Wright*
Art editor *Claire Legemah*
Managing editor *Sean Moore*
Picture researcher *Jo Walton*
Production controller *Alison Jones*

First American Edition, 1995
2 4 6 8 10 9 7 5 3 1

Published in the United States by
Dorling Kindersley Publishing, Inc.
95 Madison Avenue, New York,
New York 10016

Published in Great Britain by
Dorling Kindersley Limited.

Library of Congress CIP Data
Beckett, Wendy.
Meditations on silence / by Wendy Beckett.
1st American ed. p. cm.
ISBN 0-7894-0180-0
1.Silence--Religious aspects--Meditations.
2. Painting--Appreciation. I. Title.
BL628.2.B43 1995
179'.9--dc20 95-11883 CIP

Color reproduction by GRB Edtirice s.r.l.
Printed and bound in Hong Kong by Imago.

# CONTENTS

# PROFOUND SILENCE

THE CAPACITY FOR SILENCE – a deep, creative awareness of one's inner truth – is what distinguishes us as human. All of us, however ordinary or flawed, have at heart a seemingly boundless longing for fulfillment, and it is their consciousness of this that makes Rembrandt's portraits so beautiful. The *Woman with a Pink* is lost in the depths of her private reflections. Her dark background is symbolically unimportant, lending greater expression to the soft brightness that plays upon her face. Visibly silent, she is explicitly encountering the mystery of being human. She does not contemplate the carnation (the "pink"), usually an emblem of love, but looks within, in silence, quiet and engrossed.

*Woman with a Pink, 1665-9, Rembrandt Van Rijn*
*36¼ x 29¼ in (92 x 74.5 cm) oil on canvas*
*Metropolitan Museum of Art, New York*

# RELATIVE SILENCE

PERUGINO'S FACES ARE often too sweet, too other-worldly, but this little picture is unforgettable. It is only in the most technical sense *St. Mary Magdalen*, and Perugino has blazoned her name in embroidered capitals across her tunic as if in wry recognition of this. What she is is a young girl, silent indeed, but as yet unprepared to accept the seriousness of living inwardly. She floats on the surface of her spirit, pensive but not committed. This is so relative a silence that it has little transformative power. It is that easy silence, of which the most accessible form is the daydream. Real silence is both supremely simple and yet not easy. It draws us into a dimension always open to those who will allow themselves to be centered. But centring bars us from many irrelevances in which we take a guilty pleasure: Perugino's little beauty is not yet ready for the light.

*St. Mary Magdalen (cropped), c.1500, Pietro Perugino*
*18¹/₂ x 13¹/₂ in (47 x 34 cm), oil on wood panel*
*Pitti Palace, Florence*

# A Way Through

LIFE SEEMS SIMPLER if we blot out awareness of its mystery, but such a life is an impoverished one. There is a dimension to ourselves, the most essential dimension, which it is folly to ignore. Patricia Wright's *Gate* is a delicate image of this. She shows us the complexities of a normal existence – lines in confusion, with hints of gridded order behind, to which we are not privy. As we move to the center, the lines grow ever more clotted and chaotic: who can ever understand the meaning of events that make up our conscious experience – in relationships, in business, or whatever? But the swirls of events are the context wherein is held the gate. It is a real but shadowy presence, a way through, a possibility. If we allow silence to open up within, we shall see the gate and be free to open it.

*Gate, 1993, Patricia Wright*
*9 x 9 in (23 x 23 cm), acrylic on paper*
*Private collection*

# INTO THE LIGHT

THE GATE THAT SILENCE opens up within us leads to light. Light exposes with an almost merciless radiance and, in the exposure, reveals the beauty of the real. Vermeer always painted this holy light. He may seem, on first looking, to be depicting a young woman, standing at a half-opened window, wrapped peacefully in her own thoughts, but she and her surroundings are merely the pretext. Vermeer's intensity is focused on the light itself, only visible to us as it falls on the material world. It shimmers on the woman's white headdress, glimmers on the copper of the jug and ewer, gleams with ineffable softness on the walls. Every element in the painting celebrates the presence of light, revealing and transforming. No painter has ever believed more totally in light than Vermeer – and hence the profoundly contemplative nature of his art.

*Young Woman with a Water Jug, c.1662, Jan Vermeer*
*17⅞ x 16½ in (46 x 42 cm), oil on canvas*
*Metropolitan Museum of Art, New York*

# MANIFESTATION

ONLY THE ABSTRACT artist can attempt to show us light in itself, free from any material context. This is pure silence, the experience removed from the concrete and celebrated as a transforming peace. Epiphany is a Greek word meaning manifestation, a revelation of glory. We are not meant to understand Natkin's picture, any more than we are meant to intellectualize during our silences. We enter into silence to let the holiness of mystery take possession of us. We do this not in the absence of thought, but beneath thought. Natkin shows us infinite shades of color, a constantly receding radiance. The longer that we gaze at it, the more we "see": not in understandable images but in pure experience of chromatic brightness. This undifferentiated experience is integral to silence.

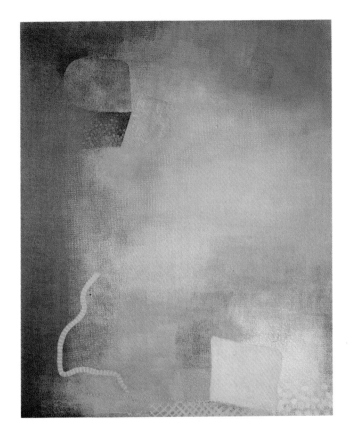

*Epiphany, 1990, Robert Natkin*
*70 x 50 in (178 x 127 cm), acrylic on canvas*
*Private collection*

# THE STILL MIND

WHAT MATTERS IS not silence itself, which can be merely physical, but what we do within it. The great mystic Teresa of Avila called the mind a clacking mill that goes on grinding. This is the nature of the mind: to have thoughts. We can indeed still the mind, through intense psychic application, but such application – directed wholly to the self – may be so self-satisfying as to abnegate its very purpose. The purpose of silence is a directed stillness, which receives rather than acts. There is only one state of perfect freedom from thought, and that is ecstasy. Raphael's St. Catherine is rapt, lost to everything but her comprehension of God. She leans carelessly on the wheel of her martyrdom, which curves inexorably toward the heavens where she truly lives. This rapturous state is pure gift and not for our seeking. (As soon as we seek, self comes in and renders such efforts useless.)

*St. Catherine of Alexandria (cropped), c.1507, Raphael*
*28 x 21¾ in (71.5 x 53.5 cm), oil on wood panel*
*National Gallery, London*

# A RICH EMPTINESS

BEN JOHNSON HAS taken as his special theme the way light shines on emptiness. *The Queen's House, Greenwich* is utterly still, utterly bare to our gaze. We are presented with a silent vista, not so much an invitation to advance through the arch and onward as to stand motionless and simply experience. There is almost tangibly no sound, and what Johnson manages to suggest implicitly is that the richness is in the standing still, the nonacting. Just to be there, to take our smallness into this classical poise, is to become more potentially our true selves; it is not outer reality that silence reveals, but our own innerness. Silence is essentially a surrender to the holiness of the divine mystery, whether we use these words or not. An atheist, calming his or her spirit in the peace of silence, is irradiated by the same mystery, anonymous but transforming. We are to listen. To what? To silence.

*Queen's House, Greenwich II, 1978, Ben Johnson*
*96 x 47¹/₄ in (244 x 120 cm), acrylic on canvas*
*Private collection*

# MEDITATIVE SILENCE

THERE ARE LAYERS of silence. Van der Weyden's Magdalen is deeply silent, but she is reading. Her mind is active, and willed into activity. This, then, is a mitigated silence, since we are only receptive to the thoughts of what we are reading. The Magdalen is obviously reading the scriptures, and meditating on what she reads, but her silence can only be between passages of reading and will be concerned with those passages. If we do not read with intervals of silent reflection, we will understand only part of what we read. This is a fractured silence, good but imperfect. We all need to read, to keep our spirit alert, to have an inner texture, as it were, that can respond to the absolutes of pure soundlessness, but this chosen, meditative layer, is the least significant.

*The Magdalen Reading (detail), c.1445, Rogier Van der Weyden*
*24¹⁄₄ x 21¹⁄₂ in (61.5 x 54.5 cm), oil on wood panel*
*National Gallery, London*

# A PARADOX

SILENCE IS A PARADOX, intensely there and, with equal intensity, not there. The passivity of silence is hard to explain, since in one respect it is intensely active. We hold ourselves in a condition of surrender. We choose not to initiate, nor to cooperate with our mental processes. Yet from this passivity arises creativity. This mysterious liberation from all commonplace worldly demands is exemplified in Rebecca Salter's

abstractions, which have been compared to gazing at a waterfall. Salter seems to have painted silence itself: the work is both alive and moving, and yet still, so that the eye wanders absorbed and yet patternless, through and among the shapes before us. There is nothing to say, nothing even to experience in any words that sound impressive, yet the looking never wearies. This is a rough image, in its very image-lessness, of the bliss of silence.

*Untitled H30 (diptych), 1993 Rebecca Salter 54 x 96 in (137 x 244 cm) Acrylic and canvas Jill George Gallery, London*

# DESIRING SILENCE

PROFOUND SILENCE IS NOT something we fall into casually. This may indeed happen, and a blessed happening it is, but normally we choose to set aside a time and a place to enter into spiritual quietness. (Those who never do this, or who shrink from it, run a very grave risk of remaining only half fulfilled as humans). Craigie Aitchison's view of Holy Island pares this choice down to its fundamental simplicities. Brown earth, blue sea, red sky, Holy Island a stony gray lit by glory. There is a small ship to take us across, if we choose to ride in it. There are no fudging elements here: all is clear-cut. This is not silence itself but rather the desire for silence. Silence, being greater than the human psyche, cannot be compressed within our intellectual categories; it will always elude us. But the desire to be silent, the understanding of the absolute need for it: this is expressed in Aitchison's wonderful diagram of life within the sight of the holy.

*Holy Island from Lamlash, 1994, Craigie Aitchison*
*42 x 38 in (106.5 x 96.5 cm), oil on canvas*
*Thomas Gibson Fine Art Ltd, London*

# CLEANSING

ENTERING INTO SILENCE is like stepping into cool clear water. The dust and debris are quietly washed away, and we are purified of our triviality. This cleansing takes place whether we are conscious of it or not: the very choice of silence, of desiring to be still, washes away the day's grime. Courbet's soft-flowing stream disappears into the darkness of the cliff, a happy image of the mystery to which we surrender ourselves when we accept the balm of silence.

*The River Brême, 1865, Gustave Courbet
29 x 36¹/2 in (73.5 x 92.5 cm), oil on canvas
Musée des Beaux-Arts et d'Archéologie
Besançon, France*

# TRUE PERSPECTIVE

OUR WORLD MAY BE one of struggle or even combat. It was at the Battle of Issus that Alexander the Great changed the course of the then-world's history, yet how small and remote it is in Altdorfer's painting. We are above it all, distanced by the immensities of time and space, looking down from a heavenly height at the tiny passions of those who fight. From here even the mountains seem small and inconsiderable, and the only real event is in the skies, where light encounters darkness – the daily and fore-destined battle we call dawn and sunset. Silence, distancing us, shakes our life into perspective, and we learn not to care for what is ephemeral and insignificant.

*The Battle of Issus (detail), 1529, Albrecht Altdorfer*
*62$^{1}/_{2}$ x 47$^{1}/_{2}$ in (158.5 x 120.5 cm), oil on wood panel*
*Alte Pinakothek, Munich*

# AMID THE CHAOS

To KNOW WHAT matters and what does not is the lesson that we long to be taught. Mondrian's *Still Life with Ginger Pot II* shows us a geometrical tangle of incoherent lines, which might or might not have a meaning. But at the center of all this, pure, rounded,

*Still Life with Ginger Pot II, 1911-12, Piet Mondrian*
*36 x 47¹/₄ in (91.5 x 120 cm), oil on canvas*
*Haags Gemeentemuseum, The Hague, Holland*

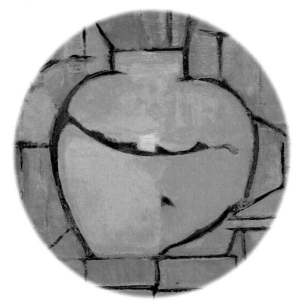

and still, gleams the pot, the one satisfying certainty amid the existential chaos. It is only when we are still, when we open up to our inner reality, that the things in our life fall into coherence for us. We do not necessarily have to think this out: silence makes the order plain. But instead we quieten our restless minds, and then rise to find that we now see the essential.

# SILENCE AND TIME

A QUICK GLANCE AT *Three Grays* and we might walk away, thinking it drab and over regulated. A slower glance, and the painting reveals an infinitude of subtle hues and shifting verticals. Its beauty, like so much else we see, reveals itself only in time. Silence is making-friends-with-time. It does not fight it or waste it; it refuses to run after it. Silence floats free with time, letting the pattern of the moments unfold at its own pace. It is a way of becoming free, not only for the practical advantage of being able to see the beauty in what is gray, for example, but at a far deeper level. In silence we break the hold time has on us, and accept in practice that our true home is in eternity.

*Three Grays, 1987, Yuko Shiraishi*
*72 x 54 in (183 x 137 cm), oil on canvas*
*Edward Totah Gallery, London*

# FORTITUDE

OTTICELLI'S LOVELY *Fortitude* is armed: she maintains a waiting silence. This is silence as attentiveness, a gathering together of one's forces. *Fortitude* is not at all on the attack. She sits amid her flowing drapery and holds her weapon at rest. But she is alert in her resting. Her feet are poised to spring into action, and her arms and bosom are protected by armor. There is nothing casual about silence. In its peace it is productive. It prepares us for whatever is to come. Our bodily eyes may (or may not) be shut, but the eyes of the spirit are wide open and watchful. Silence is, in itself, armor.

*Fortitude, c.1470, Sandro Botticelli*
*65³/₄ x 34¹/₄ in (167 x 87 cm), tempera on wood panel*
*Uffizi Gallery, Florence*

# BEYOND BABEL

WHAT SILENCE principally armors us against is Babel: the endless foolish chatter, words used to confound thought, words misused to ward off friendship or attachments, words as occupation. The biblical Babel was a metaphor for the loss of human ability to communicate as a consequence of the rise of different languages; but the foreignness of other tongues is a smoke screen. To express what one means, and to hear what another means: this is a rare thing. Babel is profoundly destructive of our energies, as Bruegel so splendidly shows. This monstrous tower is consuming all who labor on or near it. We have an absolute need for quiet, for the heart's wordless resting on God.

*The Tower of Babel, c.1563, Pieter Bruegel the Elder*
*44¹/₂ x 61 in (114 x 155 cm), tempera on wood panel*
*Kunsthistoriches Museum, Vienna*

# A STILL LIFE

IN A CRYSTAL VASE, bathed in sunlight, Manet's *White Lilac* has no function except to exist. In the last year of his life, wretchedly shortened through illness, Manet painted several of these vases of simple flowers. Their singleness of being must have moved him and perhaps consoled him amid the anxieties and anguishes of his own pain-filled days. Silence has something of this function: a simplifying, a beautifying. It reminds us that we have only to be still and let the waters of grace refresh us and the sunlight of peace shine upon us.

*White Lilac, 1882-3, Edouard Manet*
*21¼ x 16½ in (54 x 42 cm), oil on canvas*
*National Gallery, Berlin*

# AWAITING SILENCE

THIS ENCHANTING miniature shows a young woman, alone in the night, awaiting her lover. All nature seems to wait with her, and the moon swings in the sky like an expectant hammock. It is this confident expectation that makes silence possible. We are actively waiting. What (or whom) we are all waiting for must be a personal recognition that each of us has to make alone. But silence is only possible if we trust in it.

*Awaiting the Beloved, 1820-25, Indian Miniature*
*10 x 6³/₄ in (25 x 17 cm), gouache on paper*
*Victoria and Albert Museum, London*

# THE BLISS OF SILENCE

THIS TILE STOOD FOR centuries on the ridge of the roof of a Chinese temple or perhaps home. It shows a Lohan, a Buddhist saint, a monk who has "made it": attained pure bliss. Weather-beaten by all the seasons, this Lohan expresses most beautifully the bliss of silence. He has that inner smile that tells of an immensity of peace. His silence has been totally fruitful; he has found true fulfillment. He smiles, not at us, nor for any specific purpose, but because his quiet has brought him to this state of gentle smiling. He is where we desire silence one day to bring us all.

*Buddhist Ridgetile, China*
*Late Ming dynasty*
*15 in (38 cm), glazed pottery*
*Alistair Sampson Ltd*

# I N D E X

# PICTURE CREDITS

**Endpapers** Reproduced by courtesy of the Trustees of the National Gallery, London
**p5** Reproduced by courtesy of the Trustees of the National Gallery, London
**p7** Collection Haags Gemeentemuseum - The Hague/©1995 ABC/ Mondrian Estate/Holtzman Trust. Licensed by ILP
**p9** The Metropolitan Museum of Art, Bequest of Benjamin Altman, 1913 (14.40.622) ©1991 By The Metropolitan Museum of Art
**p11** Palazzo Pitti, Florence/ Bridgeman Art Library
**p13** Private Collection
**p15** Metropolitan Museum of Art, New York/Giraudon
**pp16-17** Courtesy of the artist
**p19** Reproduced by courtesy of the Trustees of the National Gallery, London
**p21** Courtesy of the artist
**pp22-23** Reproduced by courtesy of the Trustees of the National Gallery, London
**pp24-25** Courtesy of Jill George Gallery, London
**p27** Courtesy of Thomas Gibson Fine Art Ltd
**pp28-29** Besançon (France), Musée des Beaux-Arts et d'Archéologie. Cliché Ch. Choffet
**p31** Alte Pinakothek, Munich/ Joachim Blauel - Artothek
**pp32-33** Collection Haags

Gemeentemuseum - The Hague/©1995 ABC/ Mondrian Estate/Holtzman Trust. Licensed by ILP
**p35** Courtesy of Edward Totah Gallery
**p37** Uffizi Gallery, Florence/Scala
**pp38-39** Kunsthistorisches Museum, Vienna
**p41** Staatliche Museen zu Berlin, Preußicher Kulturbesitz Nationalgalerie
**p42** By Courtesy of the Board of Trustees of the Victoria and Albert Museum
**p43** Courtesy of Alistair Sampson Ltd

## JACKET PICTURE CREDITS

Style of Orcagna
*Altarpiece: The Coronation of the Virgin, with Adoring Saints (detail)*

Lochner
*Saints Matthew, Catherine of Alexandria and John the Evangelist (detail)*

Style of Orcagna
*Small Altarpiece: The Crucifixion (detail)*

Reproduced by courtesy of the Trustees of the National Gallery, London